Florence NiGhTinGaLE

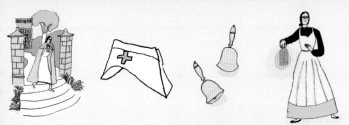

 Life Stories

Florence
NiGhTinGaLE

by Kitson Jazynka

Illustrated by Charlotte Ager

Senior Editor Allison Singer
Senior Designer Joanne Clark

Senior Editors Marie Greenwood, Roohi Sehgal
Editor Abhijit Dutta
Art Editor Roohi Rais
Jacket Coordinator Issy Walsh
Jacket Designer Dheeraj Arora
DTP Designers Mrinmoy Mazumdar, Sachin Gupta
Picture Researcher Aditya Katyal
Pre-Producer David Almond
Producer Basia Ossowska
Managing Editors Laura Gilbert, Monica Saigal
Deputy Managing Art Editor Ivy Sengupta
Managing Art Editor Diane Peyton Jones
Delhi Team Head Malavika Talukder
Creative Director Helen Senior
Publishing Director Sarah Larter

Subject Consultant Holly Carter-Chappell
Literacy Consultant Stephanie Laird

First American Edition, 2019
Published in the United States by DK Publishing
1450 Broadway, New York, New York, 10018
Copyright © 2019 Dorling Kindersley Limited

DK, a Division of Penguin Random House LLC
19 20 21 22 23 10 9 8 7 6 5 4 3 2 1
001–311452–Apr/2019

A catalog record for this book is available from the Library of Congress.
ISBN: 978-1-4654-7843-6 (Paperback)
ISBN: 978-1-4654-7844-3 (Hardcover)

DK books are available at special discounts when purchased in bulk for sales promotions,
premiums, fund-raising, or educational use. For details, contact:
DK Publishing Special Markets, 345 Hudson Street,
New York, New York 10014
SpecialSales@dk.com

Printed and bound in China

A WORLD OF IDEAS:
SEE ALL THERE IS TO KNOW

www.dk.com

Dear Reader,

When we learn about the life of a famous person, we often only hear the headlines. Florence Nightingale is known to many simply as the "Lady with the Lamp."

However, the more life stories you read or hear about a person, the better you get to know them. Florence cared for others (including many animals) from the time she was very young. She also had a habit of speaking her mind, standing up for herself, and changing things for the better. The lamp, which she carried as she cared for soldiers at night during a war, was just a small part of her story.

In some ways, Florence was a very private person. On the other hand, she loved sharing what she learned. I think she'd be glad to know you're reading about her life. She'd likely be pleased if her story inspires you to use your voice for good, to care for others—especially those in need—and to work hard to achieve your goals no matter what challenges get in the way.

Kitson Jazynka

The life of...
Florence
Nightingale

"Lady WITH THE lamp"

The gloomy Barrack Hospital in Scutari, a district of Istanbul, Turkey, probably wasn't like any hospital you might have visited.

Dust, dirt, and death filled the large building, which was crowded with sick and injured men. War reporters sent reports home to England of the terrible conditions and of soldiers dying from wounds, cold, and hunger.

It was 1854. The Crimean War had been underway for about a year. When Russia had invaded Turkish-owned lands, French and British soldiers had rushed over to join the war and help defend the small country.

---

what are war reporters?

Journalists sent to war to observe and ask questions. They share what they learn about the people and events of the war through news sources in their home country.

Inside the Barrack Hospital, another war raged—a battle to keep wounded and ill British soldiers from dying. Yet only the rats and the fleas seemed to thrive. Soldiers lay in misery, squeezed into endless rows. Some didn't even have beds, and many were without blankets or bandages.

In the midst of these awful conditions, one remarkable nurse looked past the fleas and filth and made change. That remarkable nurse was Florence Nightingale.

Originally built for Turkish soldiers, the Barrack Hospital was massive. It had four towers, long hallways, and a big courtyard.

At the Barrack Hospital, Florence organized and directed. She scrubbed and sanitized. She took notes. She chased rats. She saved lives and, in doing so, altered the course of medical history. However, when she first arrived in Scutari with her team of 38 women nurses, it was as if she faced a brick wall: an all-male medical team who did not think women could help them. She soon changed that.

Stories of Florence's heroic efforts traveled back to England through the soldiers' letters and the war reporters' newspaper articles. These included stories about the care and compassion Florence and her team of nurses showed.

A portrait of Florence carrying a lamp while checking on soldiers in a darkened hospital ward made a sensation in a popular newspaper back home. The newspaper had called her the "Lady with the Lamp." Soon she was one of the first British celebrities, and one of the most famous people of her time.

Florence made nightly rounds at the Barrack Hospital. She tended to the soldiers, listening to their concerns and calming them so they could sleep.

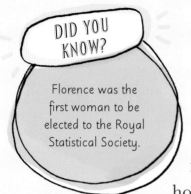

Florence was much more than just a lady with a lamp, though. She was unstoppable and strong. She fought for major improvements in how hospitals work, transformed nursing into a respected profession for women, and created the first scientifically based nursing school. A brilliant and determined student, she studied hard and learned all she could.

Florence shared what she learned about health care in the books, reports, and letters she wrote throughout her life. Beyond her writing, she also collected data and statistics. She used these to find trends in the numbers. Then, to share what she discovered, she created charts and graphs so others could better understand how health care was changing.

What are statistics?

Facts or pieces of information that help people understand something. Florence used statistics to help people understand the importance of health care.

VICTORIAN AGE

Queen Victoria ruled Britain from 1837 to 1901, a time when the country was growing in both population and wealth. Towns and cities prospered because of advancements in education, politics, health care, and technology. Women were expected to meet strict standards of perfection. They tried to emulate, or copy, Queen Victoria who—with Prince Albert and their nine children—looked to have ideal family values.

Florence's story takes place in the Victorian age. Women had few rights and opportunities. They were only said to be "accomplished" if they could play music, sing, dance, and draw. Little else was expected of them.

Florence would not let that stop her from following her dreams. How did she accomplish so much, given the limitations of her time and the terrible challenges of the Crimean War? It all began with her curious mind.

2

Early childhood

It was well after dark and time to snuff the candle, but young Florence, known to her family as "Flo," could not bear to close her book.

It was the early 1830s. Florence might have been 10 or 11 years old. Her governess, Miss Christie, said it was time for bed, but how could Flo sleep when there was so much to learn? Maybe she was reading a book that would help her identify the shells and jellyfish specimens she loved to collect on the beach, or maybe it was a puzzle book full of math riddles. Unable to tear herself away from the pages she craved, she pulled the book under her bedcover, along with

---

What is a governess?

A woman employed to teach and care for children in the home.

her small candle. She was careful to keep the hot flame from touching the bedsheets.

Her bed didn't catch fire, but when Miss Christie returned to check on Florence and saw the candle, she scolded the girl anyway. The governess might have also wondered out loud why the stubborn, strong-willed child couldn't just follow the rules like her older sister.

Born May 12, 1820, Florence was named after the city where she was born. Her wealthy and well-traveled English parents, William and Frances "Fanny" Nightingale, had been on an extended trip to Italy at the time of their second daughter's birth.

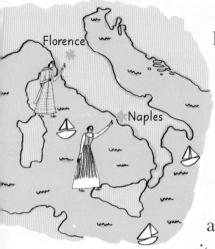

Florence's father's original
last name was Shore. He
changed it to Nightingale
five years earlier after he
took over his great-uncle
Peter Nightingale's estate.
Flo's sister, Parthenope, just
one year older than Flo, was
also named after the Italian
city of her birth. ("Parthenope"
is from the old Greek word for Naples.) She was
often called "Parthe" or "Pop."

The sisters spent their early years living in the
family's two homes in England—a country
home in Derbyshire called Lea Hurst and a
large, formal home closer to London called
Embley Park. Their lives were full of parties,
pampered pets, and important people.

Young Florence was very precise. In 1826,
for example, at only six years old, she wanted to
know if her nightly prayers were being answered.
To confirm, she conducted an experiment by
carefully noting her requests and dates.

Florence's mother, Fanny, cared very much about discipline. She once rewarded Florence with a gift for going a week without being disobedient. In a letter to her mother, nine-year-old Flo promises to behave, including taking "half an hour's walk before dinner," going to bed "in proper time," and visiting poor people to "take care of those who are sick."

Florence always asked a lot of questions about the world, and she loved to record and organize the information she learned. On a trip to the newly opened Zoological Society in London when she was 12, she made a list of the animals she saw, including two leopards, two bears, two parrots, and a lion, among others.

Florence loved to search the beach at low tide and make notes about the size and types of shells and other treasures she found, like a favorite blue jellyfish specimen she described in a letter to her grandmother as "large as half a tea tray." She also recorded the conditions of people and animals around her, such as a cow in a nearby pasture that had an ongoing bad cough.

Florence cared deeply for animals. She had many pets—such as a pony named Peggie and dogs named Peppercorn, Teazer, and Captain— but she especially liked birds. She once nursed back to health an injured pigeon, and as he was recovering, he would land on Florence's knee to be fed.

As an upper-class Victorian girl, Florence was expected to do charity work alongside her mother and sister. Florence had a soft spot for anyone who was suffering, so she helped with enthusiasm. She visited the poor near Lea Hurst and, later, Embley Park. Leaving their fine carriage in the village and walking among the houses, Florence and her mother and sister would deliver fresh eggs from their chicken house and fresh bread. They would also care for the sick.

Miss Christie had been Flo and Parthe's governess since they were about seven and eight years old. She had taught them math, reading, music, and needlework. When Miss Christie left the Nightingales to get married, Florence's parents hired a teacher to continue the girls' studies in music and drawing.

At the time, most girls weren't educated beyond these skills, but Flo and Parthe's father wanted his daughters to have the best education possible. He taught them many other subjects, such as science, history, and advanced math.

Parthe, typical of many girls during the Victorian period, took more interest in helping her mother arrange flowers, do needlework projects, and throw parties. Carefree and creative, she also loved to sketch and write poetry. She tolerated her often-bossy younger sister and admired her more academic gifts.

Florence was hungry for knowledge and eager to learn. She had little patience for socializing or sewing.

Instead, she was a girl of ideas and action. She knew that having knowledge gave her the ability to be independent—or at least she hoped it one day would.

Florence spent the rest of her younger years doing what she called "cultivating my intellect." Her determination to learn and to be herself despite what society expected of her would set her apart.

Clever and rebellious

As a teen, Florence rarely found herself without a book or a notebook. Like her father, William, she was a passionate reader.

Flo still made notes and documented things and situations she had questions about, such as a relative's illness and the living conditions of the local villagers. While thoughts of ball gowns, hairstyles, and marriage distracted many girls her age, Florence devoted herself to learning.

She liked to rise well before dawn to prepare for her lessons—which usually began with her father at the breakfast table.

Florence's family had a history of activism, or doing things to bring change. Her grandfather had campaigned against slavery, and an uncle had started an animal protection society.

Florence, too, had deep empathy for those in pain. One day she spied a sheepdog on the rolling hills, or downs, near her Embley Park home. A group of children throwing rocks had hurt the dog, and its owner couldn't afford the cost of a veterinarian's help. Sixteen-year-old Flo convinced the shepherd to let her help instead. She wrapped the dog's injured leg in warm cloth to reduce swelling. Over time she nursed Cap the dog back to health, dropping in to check on him day after day. Thanks to Flo, Cap lived a long, happy life.

what is empathy? The ability to share another's feelings. Florence felt empathy for anyone who was suffering, including animals.

It wasn't long after her experience with Cap that Florence had her first thoughts of devoting her life to healing the sick. She was good at it, after all!

Most girls of her time didn't study beyond the basics, but Florence was clever and independent. Her father recognized this, and he encouraged her to think and learn. She sat for hours in her father's study and practiced languages such as French, Italian, Greek, and Latin. They also studied math and history. On many days, she and her father spent hours having philosophical debates or delighting over the wonders of physics and astronomy.

"The first idea I can recollect when I was a child was a desire to nurse the sick."

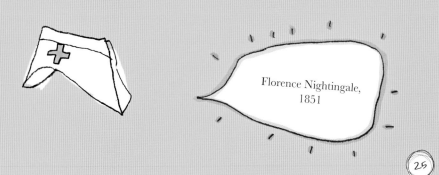

Florence Nightingale, 1851

This portrait shows Florence's love of reading books.

With her father guiding her learning, Florence earned what was considered at the time to be a "gentleman's education." She was skilled at math and enjoyed tutoring her younger cousins in tricky subjects such as algebra.

Like most Victorian girls of her age, Parthe focused her education on subjects like painting and poetry. She sometimes joined in lessons with Flo and their father, but she spent most of her time with her mother, managing the household and planning for social events.

Florence's family didn't have to work to earn money. They were already wealthy, and they had servants to do everything for them— from cooking, cleaning, and driving to dressing them and brushing their hair.

On the outside, Florence was beautiful, graceful, and stylish. She wore the latest fashions like her mother and sister and looked the part of a proper Victorian girl. However, inside, she was frustrated and restless. Her active mind, her drive to learn, and her desire to help others kept her from enjoying a simple life. She preferred to debate politics and current events with her father and the important literary and political figures that visited their luxurious homes.

VICTORIAN STYLE

Florence and Parthe, like other girls of their time and status, often wore dresses with big sleeves and skirts made of rich fabrics. They would have accessorized with ribbons, sashes, bows, bonnets, gloves, and parasols, and worn bustles and petticoats to add a pouf to their skirts. They likely wore simpler dresses at home.

Florence didn't believe that the point of a girl's upbringing should be to make herself enticing to a future husband. When her parents insisted she sit for a portrait with her sister, Flo didn't want to, but she eventually allowed her maid to dress her in a lavish pink gown. She held an embroidery project, likely as a prop to promote her as a suitable wife. She would much more likely have chosen to hold a book, as Parthe was allowed to do.

Florence craved education and to be of service to others, but the more she learned and the more she dreamed, the harder those around her worked to keep her in the role that was expected for a girl. Had Florence's "gentlemen's education" made life harder for a young woman of her time?

In the portrait, Florence is looking down instead of at the artist. Some people think she did this to show that she didn't like being the center of attention.

4

To be of **service**

In January 1837, when Florence was 16 years old, a terrible flu epidemic struck England.

Except for the cook and Florence, everyone at Embley got sick. Parthe, 17 years old at the time, had escaped the illness, as she had been staying with friends over the holidays.

Filled with purpose, Flo and the cook tended to their patients with medicinal teas, pain-relieving compounds, and hot and cold compresses. Florence wrote to her sister about the lively chaos brought on by the coughing and fevers. In one note to Parthe, she wrote, "I have killed no patients, though I have cured a few."

The following month, with her patients revived, Florence resumed her studies. While reading religious books from around the world, she had a realization that would shape the rest of her life. Florence told her parents she had felt a religious calling to help reduce human suffering. On February 7, 1837, she made a note in her personal calendar that she'd experienced a "call from God" to devote her life to be of service to others.

Her family, however, had other plans. Her mother and father were planning a trip abroad that the family would take for the next year and a half. Her parents intended for the trip to help complete their daughters' education and to "refine" them, making them into polished, proper women in society.

Florence devoted herself to charitable work more strongly than ever in the months before their departure. Late in the day, she often slipped out the door at Lea Hurst, the rich fabrics of her simple afternoon gown rustling. She'd tie her cloak, adjust her bonnet, and step into a waiting carriage. As the horses clip-clopped along the road to the village, she might have stared out the window, admiring the afternoon light cast on rippling grass in the fields, or watching a flock of blackbirds fly from a tree as she passed.

Visits to the sick had always been part of her life, thanks to her mother's commitment to charity work. Victorian women of her status usually spent time helping the poor, but Flo's devotion to the sick had taken on a greater importance since her call from God. Knowing she would soon be traveling, she worked hard, delivering food and blankets to those in need.

Only Florence's family seemed to mind that she missed their formal dinners. Her mother, carrying a lantern, would search the darkened village near Embley Park, where she often found her younger daughter at a sick person's bedside.

Soon it was time for her family's trip. In the fall of 1837, they left England on a steam packet called the *Monarch*.

OUT TO SEA

A steam packet, or steamship, such as the *Monarch* functioned a lot like a ferry. It would have had a regular route on which it delivered passengers and freight across a body of water.

After arriving in continental Europe, the family traveled in the comfort of a grand carriage designed to seat 12 people and to be pulled by three pairs of horses, most likely of a matching color and size. Their itinerary included crossing France, then visiting Italy and Switzerland, stopping at historic sites and attending parties and concerts along the way. They brought along six servants.

During the trip, Florence pondered the meaning of her religious calling. She also wrote in her journal, noting details like the distances they covered and their times of arrival and departure. She made notes about local customs, hospitals, people, and politics.

Florence paid close attention to the people she encountered along the way, such as passing soldiers, housekeepers, and villagers. Even though she may have enjoyed her family's dazzling trip, filled with extravagant balls, fancy hotels, and fine foods, she envied the people she observed. She wished she were free to work with purpose, like she saw them doing.

On their trip, Florence and her family visited the Royal Palace of Florence, a lavish palace in the city for which she was named.

Once back in England, Florence thought more and more about a career as a nurse. People in her social class considered nursing an inappropriate activity or profession. Hospitals at the time had a reputation for being dirty and overcrowded. As far as her family was concerned, Flo might as well as have told them she wanted to work as a kitchen maid.

Instead, her parents hoped she would marry. Smart, pretty, and elegant, Florence caught the attention of several eligible young bachelors, including Richard Monckton Milnes.

Richard was a smart, handsome, and well-traveled man who her parents considered to be a suitable match. Florence liked Richard, maybe even enough to consider marrying him—but marriage would mean being expected to run a household full-time.

Richard
Monckton Milnes

Florence wasn't ready to give up her dream
of becoming a nurse. In 1845, instead of
agreeing to marry Richard, she presented her
parents with a plan for her to train as a nurse
in a nearby hospital. Would they let her go?

Chapter 5

Following her **dream**

Their decision came quickly: Florence's parents would not allow their daughter to become a nurse.

They didn't want her to even think about it anymore. They believed she should focus on finding a husband and starting a family.

At 26 years old and unmarried, Florence lived at home at Embley Park. She felt trapped by the expectations of home and family, and she felt very alone in her frustrations.

She often expressed her feelings in her journal. In one entry, she wrote, "Oh, if no one has but a toothache, what remedies are invented! … But if it is something the matter with the mind … it is neither believed nor understood." It must have felt lonely and confusing to be so misunderstood, especially by her own family.

Florence studied by candlelight, learning everything she could about health care and hospitals despite knowing her parents would disapprove. She read newspapers and paid special attention to  reports about sanitation in England. She made lists and charts about illness and death. She also attended church, read religious texts, and pondered the meaning of what she believed was her religious calling to be of service.

"WATER! WATER! EVERYWHERE; AND NOT A DROP TO DRINK."

SMELLY SITUATION

Florence read reports about sanitation, or cleanliness, because the conditions in England were not good. Victorian England was known for its unpleasant smell. Horse manure and urine filled London's streets. Soot and smog filled the air. People hadn't yet figured out that a clean environment improves the health of its inhabitants.

Florence also helped her mother run Lea Hurst and Embley Park, keeping detailed records of the family's china and the servants' production of fruit jam. She kept up her work with the poor, and in the summer, she traveled to London to attend balls, operas, fancy dinners, and parties.

Of course, there was still Richard. He continued to visit her regularly. Around this time, Florence confided in someone that Richard "was there three times last month and each time funnier than the last." Florence liked and respected Richard enough to consider marrying him—but she knew that if she married, her chances of becoming a nurse would be slim. A husband would expect her to have children, run their home, and socialize. She did wonder if Richard might join her in a life of service, but it would be a very unconventional marriage.

That same year, a friend from Germany sent Florence information about a training hospital in Kaiserswerth, Germany. There, young, unmarried Christian women could get basic training in nursing or teaching. This place could be the answer to her dreams, but Florence didn't dare mention it to her family.

The hospital building and outdoor gardens at Kaiserswerth in Germany.

The following year, friends of the family invited Florence to spend the winter in Rome. There, she toured ancient churches and marveled at Michaelangelo's famous biblical paintings in the Sistine Chapel. She met people who cared about helping others like she did. One couple in particular, Sidney and Elizabeth Herbert, were interested in hospital reform. They were impressed by how much Florence knew on the subject, and they introduced her to others who shared her passion.

Florence visited the beautiful Sistine Chapel, where she admired Michaelangelo's breathtaking religious paintings.

Through her new friends, Florence learned about other respectable families that had sent their daughters to study at Kaiserswerth. Still, she dared not mention her dream of attending the training hospital in Kaiserswerth to her family, for fear they would refuse to let her go.

In the fall of 1848, Parthe planned a trip to a spa in Germany. The rest of the family, including Flo, would visit Frankfurt at the same time. However, the trip was called off at the last minute because of political turmoil in Germany. Disappointed, Florence devoted herself even more to activities such as teaching

poor children at a local school. She also loved
sitting on a low stone wall and reading under
a favorite tree at Embley Park.

Life at home was tense. Florence's family
continued to pressure her to marry Richard.
Richard himself also grew impatient with her
indecision. In private, Flo made detailed lists
of the advantages and disadvantages marriage
would bring. On the bright side, Richard was a
smart man with a kind heart. He was an author,
a poet, and a politician, and he was passionate
about the causes he believed in, such as his

concern for victims of
famine, or the shortage
of food, in Ireland.

DID YOU KNOW?

Florence sometimes
referred to Richard
as her "poetic parcel."

Florence adored
Richard in many ways and
truly enjoyed spending time
with him, but she shuddered to
think of losing her independence. She did not
want to get married if it meant giving up her
dream of nursing.

Her family had refused to let her attend
college—and now it was Flo's turn to say no.
At 29 years old and having put Richard off
for seven years, she turned down his proposal for
the very last time. She would have known that
turning down a proposal at her age meant she
would probably never marry.

Chapter 6

Family **struggles**

Florence's refusal to marry Richard upset her family. Her parents didn't understand why she was being so difficult.

Parthe wasn't happy, either—she counted on her popular sister for her social connections. Florence was depressed and confused. Had she made the wrong choice? Would she ever be a nurse, or was all this unhappiness for nothing?

Friends offered to help ease her suffering. They took her on a trip to Greece and Egypt, which included cruising the Nile River for 800 miles, but it didn't seem to improve her mood.

Nile River

ANIMAL FRIENDS

During her travels in 1850, Flo made many new animal friends. Her pack of pets included two chameleons, two tortoises, and a cicada she named Plato. In Athens, she rescued a young owl that had fallen from its nest and was being harassed by a group of children. She named the owl Athena and carried her in her pocket or on her shoulder. Athena was prone to tantrums and scratching others (she also ate Plato!), but Flo loved her and brought her back to England.

Desperate—and without her parent's consent, which was still critical even though Florence was an adult—Flo's friends took her to visit the training hospital at Kaiserswerth. It was July 31, 1850. When Florence arrived, she immediately felt at home.

During her stay, she learned about the work of each department. She visited the children's ward first and accompanied her hosts on night watches.

Conditions were unlike what Florence was used to at home. Instead of large, sophisticated meals with five or six courses served by the household staff, she ate watery soups. Without her maid, she combed her own hair.

Florence paid no attention to the meager conditions. Instead, she focused her attention on what she could do for the helpless people there who were suffering. She was inspired by the overwhelming kindness of the deaconesses who tended to patients. Florence stayed at the training hospital for two weeks and eventually left feeling brave and empowered, hoping to return as soon as possible.

"What can **an individual** do towards lifting the **load of** suffering from the **helpless** and **miserable?**"

Florence Nightingale,
c.1842

Florence returned to England. Her parents were happy to have her back, but they were unhappy she'd gone to Kaiserswerth without permission. On the trip home, Florence had drafted what would become a 32-page pamphlet to advertise Kaiserswerth to people in England who might be interested in training there. The pamphlet was published the following year, in 1851. To save her family the embarrassment, Florence did not include her name on it.

Having experienced Kaiserswerth, Florence was more determined than ever to train as a nurse. For the next year and half, however, she stayed home like a dutiful daughter and sister. Richard had announced his engagement to someone else.

MARRIAGE AND CHILDREN

Florence's parents hoped she would marry and have a son. They hoped the same for Parthe. It wasn't just because they wanted grandchildren—they needed a grandson in order to keep their fortune in the family. The law at the time meant that any money left to a daughter could pass to her husband's family if she didn't produce a male heir.

Florence, now 31, announced her desire to return to the school. Surprisingly her father didn't forbid it right away. He had noticed that other young women with similar social standing worked in hospitals. Parthe, who had also not yet married, hated the idea of her sister moving away. Her parents tried to convince Florence to work at a church and school near home. When that didn't work, they convinced her to devote the next six months of her life to being a companion to Parthe. Only then would they discuss her attending nursing school.

For those six months, the simmering unhappiness at home was awful for all of the Nightingales. Florence reflected on a phrase she'd read while studying the work of

---

What is a companion?

A person who accompanies another for travel or recreation. Flo's parents asked her to be a companion to her sometimes-lonely sister.

DID YOU KNOW?

A mill once owned by Florence's family is still in business today near Lea Hurst.

an ancient Greek playwright who had referred to an "unloving love." She felt handcuffed to her family, even though she knew they loved her.

Her mother tried to understand. Her reservations about Florence's nursing career came from concern. She wanted her daughter to have the best life possible, and for Fanny that had meant getting married and having children. The other women in their family, such as Flo and Parthe's "Aunt Mai"—their father's sister, Mary—campaigned on Flo's behalf.

Worried that things might get worse, Fanny and William agreed to let Florence return to Kaiserswerth—on three conditions. First, she must stay for only a few months. Second, she must travel to Germany and home again with her mother and sister; Fanny and Parthe would pass the time at a nearby healing spa. Third, Flo must promise to tell no one outside the family of their agreement or her plans.

Flo readily agreed to her family's terms. They concocted a story that she was overseas recovering from an illness, and Florence immediately prepared to leave.

Florence's family may have thought she wouldn't last long at Kaiserswerth. After all, before Kaiserswerth, dainty Flo had never even made herself a cup of tea or done her own hair! They hoped that because she wasn't used to wearing simple clothes, eating simple foods, or having to work, she'd soon tire of the place.

7

News FROM Scutari

Eager to fit in at Kaiserswerth, Florence traded colorful and stylish dresses from Paris for simple dresses in black, brown, and gray.

She trained in basic nursing skills, like how to observe a patient for signs of illness and dress a wound. She assisted in operations and prepared and administered medicine. She learned the value of good hospital organization and discovered the importance of cleanliness when caring for the sick. She also taught the other students reading, writing, and math, as many of them had not received the same quality of education Florence had.

What does "dress a wound" mean?

To protect a cut or injury with a clean pad or bandage in order to promote healing. Dressing their wounds is one of the ways nurses tend to their patients.

Florence is shown wearing one of her simple brown dresses in this oil painting.

Florence finally felt that her life had purpose. Her sister continued to be impatient with Flo's obsession with nursing. Parthe hoped it would be a passing fancy. Her parents, on the other hand, had softened their opinions. At Kaiserswerth, Florence received a kind letter from her mother. Fanny had written words of encouragement to her younger daughter, telling her to continue following her dream.

After four months, Fanny and Parthe were ready to leave the spa in Germany and return to England. Worried she'd never come back if they left without her, they insisted that Florence accompany them home.

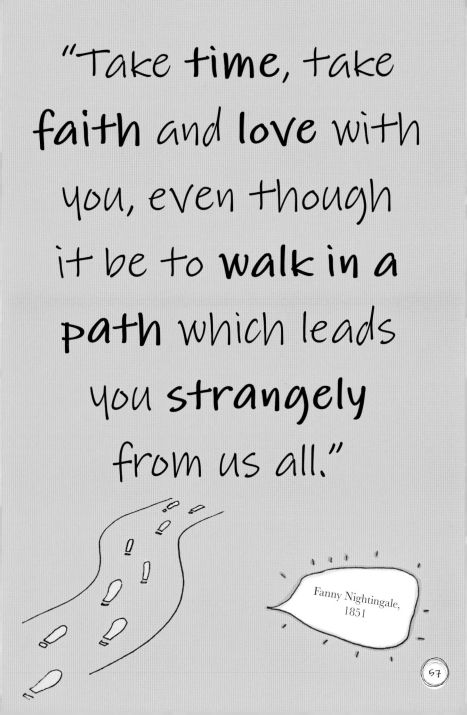

"Take time, take faith and love with you, even though it be to walk in a path which leads you strangely from us all."

Fanny Nightingale, 1851

Florence went, but something had changed. She was 33 years old now, which was considered then to be middle-aged. She would no longer let her family decide how she

DID YOU KNOW?

Parthe helped decorate Flo's first apartment on Harley Street in London. She often sent Flo gifts, such as flowers, fruits, and pheasants.

lived her life or hope for a marriage proposal. Her father decided to support his hard-working daughter despite her unusual choices. He provided her with funds for living expenses. With money of her own, she could choose what to do and where to live.

In 1853, Florence accepted a position as the superintendent at a women's hospital in London. The Institution for Sick Gentlewomen in Distressed Circumstances was a small hospital primarily for governesses with little money. Florence ran the hospital just as she and her

what is a superintendent?

The manager or leader of an activity or organization. Florence was the superintendent of a hospital in London.

sister had helped their mother run Lea Hurst and Embley Park.

One major difference between home and hospital was that the hospital had little money. Florence got to work: She balanced the budget and cut unnecessary expenses. She instructed staff to make bedcovers for the 27 patient beds out of old curtains. She purchased new linens for the place with her own money and decorated with unwanted prints and furniture from home. She started a library of books for patients with donations from her father's collection. She instructed plumbers to install pipes that would deliver hot water to each floor, so nurses wouldn't have to haul buckets of water up the stairs.

Florence also came up with a system of hand bells that the patients at the hospital could use to get the nurses' attention.

For the next 12 months, Flo worked to improve nursing care and conditions for the hospital's patients and nurses. She didn't have much free time—but when her old friend Sidney Herbert, now Secretary of State at War for the British government, asked for help, she made time. Aware of Flo's gift for documenting and organizing information, he asked Flo to help him survey hospitals in London to, among other things, document working conditions for nurses. She paid attention, took detailed notes, and, as always, learned everything she could.

A year of real-world experience sharpened Florence's focus. She found that her true passion was not only nursing, but training other women to be nurses. When offered the opportunity to become the superintendent of nurses at King's College Hospital in London, she accepted the position.

Florence accepted a job at King's College Hospital—but she would never actually work there.

However, world politics interrupted her plan. Turkey had declared war on Russia after a series of disputes. The British military had joined in to defend Turkey. Reports traveling back to London from the Crimean War had depicted gruesome hospital conditions and poor care for the sick and injured British soldiers there. With little medical care available, soldiers were dying from battle wounds, cold, hunger, and sickness. Some said more soldiers were dying in the British military hospital there than on the battlefields.

Sick and injured British soldiers arrive by the boatload at the Barrack Hospital, a military hospital in Scutari, Turkey.

THE CRIMEAN WAR

In 1853, war broke out between Turkey and Russia. Looking to expand its vast empire, Russia wanted to take over lands that were ruled by Turkey. The British and the French joined Turkey's side in 1854 after a major Russian invasion. Most of the battles of the war took place in Crimea, also known as the Crimean Peninsula, in southern Russia. The British medical hospital, the Barrack Hospital, was in Scutari. Scutari, now known as Üsküdar, is a district of the northern part of the Turkish city of Istanbul.

Florence lived in London at the time of the invasion.

RUSSIA

Crimea

UK

FRANCE

TURKEY

The Barrack Hospital was located in Scutari, a district of Istanbul, Turkey.

Florence had been reading every report she could find about the military hospital in Scutari. Her new job at King's College was waiting, but she couldn't help feeling she might be able to do more good overseas. The war was very bloody, and so many people were dying. Maybe she could help.

DID YOU KNOW?

Because she wasn't married, Florence would need her parents' permission to go to Scutari—even though she was 34 years old.

Florence wrote a letter to her friend Elizabeth Herbert. In the letter, Florence asked Elizabeth if she thought her husband, Sidney, would allow Florence to lead a team of nurses to help at the British military hospital in Scutari.

This was a very strange request, because female nurses had never worked in the British army before. In Victorian times, women were considered inferior to men when it came to their

---

what does "inferior" mean?

Lower in rank than something or someone else. Many Victorian men thought women's ability to work was inferior to their own.

ability to think and work. A woman's job, society then believed, should be to manage the home, obey their husbands, and have children. Joining the military and going to war would keep them from being able to fulfill those responsibilities.

Florence had the skills and the ambition to make a big change and do something no British woman had ever done before—but would she be allowed to help?

Nurse of war

**Flo didn't know it at the time, but Sidney was
one step ahead of his industrious friend—in
March 1854, *he* had written *her* a letter, too.**

In his letter, Sidney asked Florence to lead a group
of women nurses to Scutari—exactly what she
had hoped to do. He wrote that Florence was the
"one person in England ... capable of organizing
[and] superintending such a scheme."

Florence seized the opportunity. As she rushed
to prepare for the trip,
her only heartbreak
was the death of her
beloved owl. Athena
had died after Florence
brought her to stay at
Embley Park while she
would be in Scutari.

Scutari

TURKEY

Florence traveled to Scutari on the steamer ship *Vectis*.

Finally, on October 21, 1854, Florence and 38 nurses boarded the paddle steamer *Vectis*. It was a fast boat at the time, built for mail delivery. Through high winds and rough seas, they headed 300 miles (480 km) across the sea into a war zone.

The trip took more than two weeks. Prone to seasickness and stuck in a cramped cabin with water sloshing underfoot, Florence suffered through every high wave and could barely eat. She felt absolutely terrible, but she also felt the call of duty.

What is a war zone?

A region where a war is fought. Flo entered a war zone when she arrived in Scutari.

Florence and her team of nurses arrived to heavy rains and news of an awful battle. They got to the dock at the same time as 400 injured soldiers who were being brought in from the front lines.

At the hospital, the dead body of a Russian soldier greeted the nurses. The place was plagued with blocked drains and broken toilets. Thousands of sick or injured men lay in endless rows of mattresses crammed together. Supplies of necessities like food and bandages were dangerously low, and the existing staff had little training.

Florence and the other nurses found their rooms in the northwest corner of the ghostly building. Their tight quarters, in which some of them were to live 12 people to a room, had leaky ceilings and were inhabited by scampering rats and terrible smells.

There was no warm welcome from the doctors there, either. Women had never been part of the military, and the male doctors had very little experience taking direction from women in professional matters. With no indication that her team's help would be welcome, Florence plotted. How could she gain the confidence of the army surgeons?

The nurses busied themselves washing clothes and feeding injured soldiers. They made bandages and scrubbed floors. Some doctors absolutely refused to work with the women, and scolded their fellow medical staff members who did. Florence resolved that the nurses should not enter any of the medical wards or tend to patients unless they were specifically asked.

It didn't take long.

Within a few days of the nurses' arrival, injured and sick soldiers from the Battle of Balaklava and the Battle of Inkerman overwhelmed the harried hospital. With patients arriving daily, sometimes 700 at a time, the doctors could no longer refuse help of any kind—especially from trained nurses.

FIRST NURSING UNIFORMS

Florence insisted her nurses in Scutari wear uniforms as a means of identification and professionalism. They wore plain brown woolen dresses, linen aprons, white caps, and sashes with the words "Scutari Hospital" embroidered in red. These were the first nursing uniforms, and not everyone liked them. One nurse said that if she had known she'd have to wear it, she wouldn't have come.

The nurses cleaned wounds, tried to lower fevers, provided meals, and gave patients clean clothing. Florence's flair for organization and efficiency came in handy.

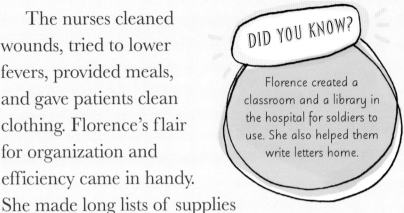

DID YOU KNOW?

Florence created a classroom and a library in the hospital for soldiers to use. She also helped them write letters home.

She made long lists of supplies that the hospital needed and documented areas of the hospital that she thought could be run in a more efficient way. She used chalk to number hospital beds so the nurses and doctors could keep track of patients. She also enlisted the soldiers' wives to assist with the laundry.

As long days turned into weeks and months, and fall turned to winter, Florence slept and ate very little. She worked 20-hour days. Every night, she wrote an update to Sidney to share and document details about the hospital's poor conditions. She lamented the lack of supplies and asked for basic things such as mops, plates, towels, forks, spoons, scissors, and linens to make bandages.

One day, Florence finally received a shipment of scrub brushes she had long been asking for. Eager to see the hospital cleaned, she had the healthiest of the patients help the nurses scrub the hospital from top to bottom.

Florence felt strongly that the soldiers should be cleaned, fed, and tended to in the right way. By Christmastime, just two months after arriving in Scutari, she had already sent some nurses home for not meeting her high standards.

The hospital lacked good procedures to receive and store food. Sometimes soldiers went hungry. Once, Florence fumed about a load of cabbage left to rot because there was no way to get it from the port to the hospital.

Relations with the male doctors remained tense at times, but Florence tried not to let them slow down her work. Focusing on the task at hand, she dedicated herself to creating a new standard of hospital care.

In this painting, Florence is shown receiving a wounded soldier on a stretcher in Scutari. Though they tried to keep the hospital running as well as possible, Florence and the other nurses were overwhelmed with patients coming in from the war.

9

War stories

Fanny and Parthe pored over the letters Florence wrote home. They distributed them to friends and family, censoring ones they thought too disgusting.

The medical descriptions of bloody stumps and other horrible war wounds were nearly too much to bear. Florence wrote in one letter that so many patients had amputated limbs, she doubted patients had an average of three limbs each. She also wrote of the smell of death and the lice that infested the soldiers' hair.

Florence's training in Kaiserswerth served her well in Scutari. Back in Germany, she had assisted in operations and stood watch over patients through the nights. She had also observed her first amputation and recorded the details in her journal:

"A beautiful operation," she wrote. "Patient suffered more in the afternoon. Cold water compresses every five minutes… Window sills decked with flower pots…"

The grisly scenes in Scutari did not prevent Florence from tending to the soldiers with a great deal of care and personal attention. During the day, she soothed her patients by talking to them. At night, she monitored them carefully. When Aunt Mai came to visit and help at the hospital, she wrote letters home telling her children how well Florence cared for her patients.

"Every poor fellow's face softens with gratitude at the sight of her."

John MacDonald,
The Times,
February 1855

A war reporter for *The Times*, a London newspaper, noticed Florence's devotion to the soldiers. In an article in February 1855, he called her the "Lady with the Lamp." "When all the medical officers have retired for the night," he wrote, "and sickness and darkness have settled down upon the miles of the sick, she may be observed, along with a little lamp, making her solitary rounds." Another London newspaper, *The Illustrated London News*, ran a similar article later that month, along with an illustration of Florence carrying a candle as she walks around checking on soldiers in the dark.

Illustration of Florence in *The Illustrated London News*

WHICH LIGHT IS RIGHT?

The lantern pictured in the famous illustration looks nothing like the lantern Florence carried. Reporters were on the scene at the Barrack Hospital, but the illustrator was in England working from descriptions. The lantern he drew was a Roman lamp. The lantern Florence really carried was a Turkish lamp called a *fanoos*, which is thought by some to be a religious symbol for "divine unity." It had a copper bottom and top, and a metal frame covered with waxed linen that held a candle. She would have held the lamp from the top or hooked it onto something to free up her hands.

Fanoos lantern

Back in England, Florence's fame grew. In addition to the war reporters' stories about the Lady with the Lamp, soldiers had been writing letters to their families at home with tales of her kindness, hard work, and the great changes she had made. Curious members of the public snuck onto the grounds of Lea Hurst and Embley Park.

In Scutari, the days and nights were still long for Florence. In one letter home, written in

March 1855, she seemed homesick. She wrote about a dream she had in which Athena visited her, bowed to her, let out a long, melancholy cry, and then flew away. "I assure you my tears followed her," she added.

Sheet music for a song about Florence

Florence had become a national hero at home in England. Fans wrote songs and poetry about her and named their ships after her. Parents of newborns around this time named their baby girls in her honor. Many of her fans began helping the poor as a result of her influence.

In late 1855, after a public meeting in London to recognize her work, there was a national appeal for a fund to help train other nurses. People raised money through concerts and other events, and soldiers who had fought in the war donated a day's pay. It was called

DID YOU KNOW?

The Nightingale Fund is still active today. Each year it helps pay for the classes of about 30 nursing students.

the Nightingale Fund, and Sidney Herbert was its honorary secretary.

Some of the money helped Florence continue her work in Scutari. She bought better medical equipment and higher-quality food, and she hired workers to clear drains. She could also afford to convert a local house into a laundry, and she enlisted help from the wives and widows of the soldiers to do the wash.

Parthe and Fanny collected newspaper clippings about Florence and wrote letters on her behalf. Promoting her sister's work gave Parthe a sense of purpose. While Florence's sister and mother enjoyed their heightened social status, her father hid away in protest, unhappy about all of the bothersome attention his family was getting.

Florence felt that stories about her had been exaggerated and that they took away focus from her real work. She referred to the glowing reports about her as "tinsel"—and, as usual, she refused to sit for a portrait.

10

Fever

In May 1855 Florence, now 35, became ill with "Crimean fever." She was as sick as any of the patients the hospital had seen.

Florence likely contracted the illness from drinking contaminated milk in Scutari. The fever had gotten so high that, though Florence kept her hair short already, her caretakers cut it even shorter to help her keep cool.

Soldiers at the hospital wept at the thought of her dying. The doctors delayed sending word home to Florence's family until they had good news. Nine agonizing days later, her fever broke. She was too weak to feed herself and could barely speak.

Florence slowly recovered in a small house away from Scutari. Some doctors are said to have tried to use her condition as an excuse

to ship her back to England, where her fans
awaited her return—but Florence, as devoted
to her work as ever, refused to go.

To cheer up her sister, Parthe sent a book
that she'd made and illustrated about the life
of Athena. Sidney Herbert sent her a dog to
better her spirits.

Despite Florence's success in making the
Barrack Hospital cleaner and more efficient,
soldiers kept dying. By early 1856, more than
4,000 soldiers had died over the winter.

That spring, officials discovered the hospital was built on a sewer. Patients had been drinking contaminated water. The area was flushed out and improved, and the number of patients dying at the hospital decreased dramatically.

On March 30, 1856, a treaty ended the Crimean War. Florence remained in Scutari until the last of her patients left the hospital. Traveling home a few months later, she used the name "Miss Smith" to avoid drawing attention. In August, she walked through the ivy-covered gate at Lea Hurst. She was still suffering the effects of her illness and exhaustion, which would plague her for the rest of her life.

What is a treaty? An agreement between countries. The Treaty of Paris ended the Crimean War.

Florence didn't like her fame, but it gave her power. Now she could more easily convince others that hospital reform was an important topic. She could make sure nursing became an important and respectable profession for women.

Florence's new projects also brought her family closer. Her mother and sister worked hard to promote her efforts. Cousins and other family members joined in to help her run the hospital she would later open.

DEVOTED SISTER

In 1858, Parthe married Sir Harry Verney, who had once asked Florence to marry him. A talented writer and painter, Parthe continued to help her sister spread her important messages. Although their relationship was often fraught with tension, they remained close throughout their lives.

Queen Victoria and Prince Albert

In September 1856, a month after she had
returned from Scutari, Florence received an
invitation. Queen Victoria of England and her
husband, Prince Albert, had taken an interest in
the welfare of the soldiers who returned from the
Crimean War. They invited Florence for a short,
formal visit.

It was a high honor. It was also not the first
time Florence had had a personal audience with
the queen. At 36 and having seen the horrors of
war, this Florence was much different than the

stylish young debutante who had stood before Queen Victoria 20 years earlier.

In their brief meeting, Queen Victoria and Prince Albert thanked Florence for her hard work. They also discussed her ideas about how to provide better care for sick and injured soldiers in times of war. A year earlier, they had given Florence a beautiful engraved brooch now called the "Nightingale Jewel." The queen also awarded Florence a large sum of money for her efforts. Florence later used the money to fund a hospital and a training school for nurses.

Florence's health was poor. She was very thin and had very short hair, unlike most women of the time. She was in pain and depressed about her health, but she was still determined to get as much work done as possible before the end of her life, which she feared might soon come.

Queen Victoria presented Florence with this jeweled brooch in 1855.

Chapter 11

Bedside

In 1858, Florence was 38 years old, and she hardly left home. It would be this way for the rest of her life.

She lived in Mayfair, a wealthy area in the West End of London near Buckingham Palace, interviewing politicians and welcoming distinguished visitors from her bed.

Bursting bookshelves and light from tall windows filled her bedroom. She wrote constantly, using a velvet-lined wood writing case. Beautifully painted, the case had been a gift in honor of her safe return after the war. It was given to her by villagers who lived

Florence's writing case

near Lea Hurst. The case had room for an ink bottle, a rack to hold pens, and multiple compartments, perhaps for stamps, sealing wax, and envelopes.

Flo's illness may have limited her physical ability, but her mind stayed sharp. No matter how poor her own health, Florence remained as determined as ever to improve the way England provided health care for its people. She worked from the comfort of her bedroom with attentive housecats for company. When she did travel, her cats often accompanied her on the train.

Florence held a strong belief that patients should not suffer. Despite not leaving the house much, she campaigned to improve England's health standards, publishing more than 200 books, reports, and pamphlets on hospital planning and organization. Many of these publications are still widely read today.

The Nightingale Training School for Nurses opened in 1860 at St. Thomas' Hospital in London. The school's reputation soon spread, and "Nightingale nurses" were requested to start new schools all over the world, including Africa, Australia, and America.

St. Thomas' Hospital in London

Florence was very sick, but she had family money to pay for help and care. She knew others in England weren't as fortunate. She believed that everyone, not just those who could afford to pay, should have medical care. Around the same time her training school opened, Florence published a book called *Notes on Nursing*. It was intended to teach people to care for their sick relatives as a way to help even the poorest citizens of England. In the book, she gives practical advice, such as that a "dark house is always an unhealthy house."

NOTES ON NURSING

More than 150 years after Florence wrote *Notes on Nursing*, nurses all over the world refer to its wisdom. The book addresses many issues and problems that nurses still confront today. Florence's words on everything from what it means to be a nurse, to the confidentiality of medical details, to dealing with infections, remain useful.

DID YOU KNOW?

During the US Civil War, from 1861 to 1865, Florence consulted for the US military on how to manage field hospitals.

Florence wanted to prevent the mistakes made during the war from happening again. She got help from leading statisticians to analyze vast amounts of detailed army data. Their research revealed that of the 18,000 British soldiers who died in the Crimean War, 16,000 of the deaths resulted from diseases spread by poor sanitation that could have been prevented.

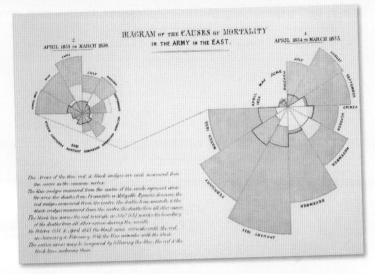

Florence's coxcomb diagram helps show that more soldiers in the war died from disease than from injuries.

Knowing government officials might not make time to read lengthy statistical reports, Florence made a diagram that displays the data in a visual way so it can be easily understood. Drawn with pen and ink, Florence's diagram illustrates the poor sanitation in British hospitals during the Crimean War. It shows that more patients had died from disease than from their war wounds. Her creative and easy-to-read diagram, which is now called either a "coxcomb" or a "rose" diagram, helped government officials make medical reform a priority.

Florence spent much of her later life in bed at her home in Mayfair, London.

Florence continued to work from her bed for decades. Despite her illness, her aim was to keep improving the management of health throughout the army. She often worked before dawn by the light of a candle, with her writing desk on her lap. Florence wrote hundreds of letters each month—more than 13,000 letters in total over the years—and sometimes spent as many as 12 hours a day writing.

Florence was always surrounded by her cats. She had as many as 17 cats at one point. They sometimes left inky paw prints across her letters.

LIFETIME OF LETTERS

We know a lot about Florence's history in part because thousands of her letters—along with journals and random notes and scribbles—have been saved. In 1895, she wrote that she had enough letters in her drawers and stuffed under sofas "to cover Australia." At one point, fearing her writings would be misunderstood, she asked her family to burn all of her 80 years of letters and manuscripts after her death. Luckily for us, she changed her mind!

In August 1910, at age 90, Florence seemed not to feel well, but she recovered and was in good spirits. A week later, however, she died at her home in Mayfair. Her parents had died years before, and she had outlived her sister, too.

Florence's remaining family was offered an elaborate funeral for her in Westminster Abbey, a famous church in London that is the site of royal coronations and other distinguished ceremonies. However, Florence had asked for a quiet and modest remembrance.

Her family respected her wishes. Florence was buried alongside the graves of other family members in East Wellow, Hampshire, near her childhood home at Embley Park.

Florence is buried in the graveyard at St. Margaret's Church in East Wellow, Hampshire, UK.

Chapter 12

Remembering Florence

Today, many people know Florence Nightingale only as the "Lady with the Lamp" who cared for injured and sick soldiers in the middle of a war.

That part of the story is true—and it's what made her famous—but her heroics weren't limited to stories from the Crimean War. Florence spent most of her life caring for others and fighting for what she believed to be right. She expanded opportunities for women for generations to come and worked to improve health care for all. She transformed nursing into a respected profession. She was a pioneer in displaying health care information, using statistics so others could understand her observations.

What is a pioneer?	Someone who is the first person to explore a new area. Florence was a pioneer in the field of nursing.

Florence worked to lessen the suffering of others, from dying soldiers and patients to the medical staff working in awful conditions. She was passionate about her work as a nurse, and she overcame just about every challenge that she faced.

Although she was raised in a wealthy family, Florence's life was not easy. From the time she was young, those closest to her struggled to understand why she wouldn't conform to what society expected of a woman of her status. Florence could never have known then she would work for 50 years to reform standards of public health in England—or that, in doing so, she would save so many lives.

In 1881, the Army Nursing Service was established, which meant that nurses were now officially part of the British military.

DID YOU KNOW?

International Nurses Day is celebrated every year on May 12— Florence's birthday.

"**Nursing** is an **art...**
it requires as
exclusive a **devotion,**
as **hard** a
preparation,
as any painter's
or sculptor's work."

Florence Nightingale,
1859

Florence's legacy had enormous impact even after her death. Over a century later, people remain interested in Florence's story. She is remembered with memorial statues, buildings, schools, and hospital wards that bear her name. Walking through the Florence Nightingale Museum, which sits at the site of the original Nightingale Training School for Nurses in London, a person will find more than 2,000 artifacts from her life. These include personal belongings, such as the slate she used as a child for her lessons. Visitors can also see her shawl and the tin foot-warmer she used during long, cold carriage trips.

Medicine chest used by Florence during the war in Crimea

Cross worn by Florence in her youth

Even little Athena the owl's body rests at the Florence Nightingale Museum, to remind visitors of Flo's affection for animals.

Every year, Westminster Abbey holds a ceremony in Florence's honor. The service celebrates nurses and remembers Florence's example of compassion, care, and commitment to training. As part of the ceremony, a "Florence Nightingale lamp" is carried through the abbey.

The International Committee of the Red Cross, an organization that helps people during times of disaster, honors her memory with the

Florence Nightingale Medal. It is the highest international honor that a nurse can receive, and it recognizes those nurses who have set themselves apart by showing courage and creativity in times of peace or war. More than 1,300 nurses from all over the

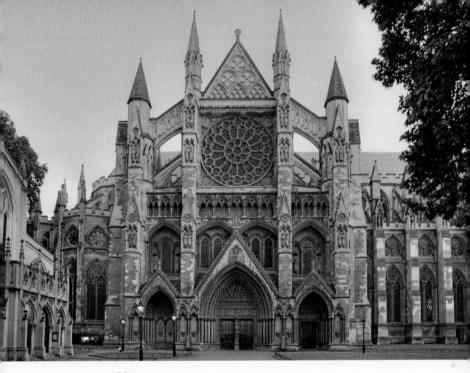

Westminster Abbey

world have received the medal. Like Florence, they overcame serious challenges in situations that included natural disasters and conflict.

During her life, Florence Nightingale showed great courage and confidence, but she also had many frustrations and disappointments. Her ideas and her hard work make up her life story, and they also changed the life stories of many women who would enter the field of medicine in the future.

A nurse serves as "Lamp Carrier" during a special ceremony at Westminster Abbey to celebrate nursing and Florence's life. Because of her legacy, the lamp has become an international symbol of nursing.

Florence's actions still touch millions of people, such as the nurses who work in the military today, or the patients who benefit from good sanitation conditions in hospitals. Perhaps Florence's greatest achievement, though, is never giving up on her life's goals even when challenges—such as her family's opposing beliefs, a terrible war, or her own health—got in her way. "Live life when you have it," she once said. "Life is a splendid gift—there is nothing small about it."

Florence's
family tree

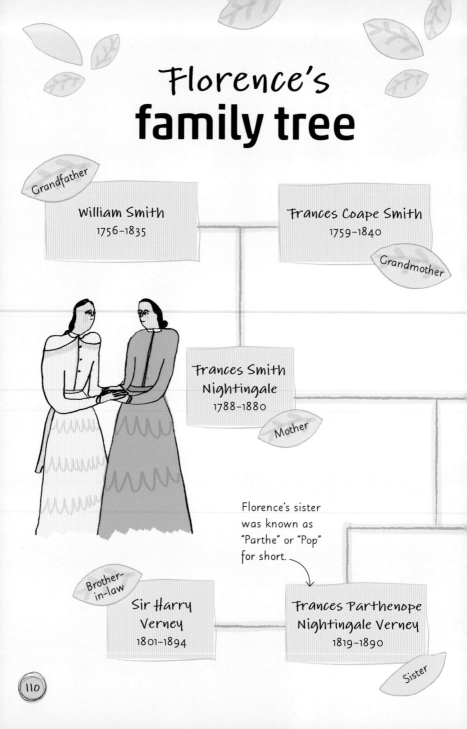

Grandfather

William Smith
1756–1835

Frances Coape Smith
1759–1840

Grandmother

**Frances Smith
Nightingale**
1788–1880

Mother

Florence's sister
was known as
"Parthe" or "Pop"
for short.

Brother-
in-law

**Sir Harry
Verney**
1801–1894

**Frances Parthenope
Nightingale Verney**
1819–1890

Sister

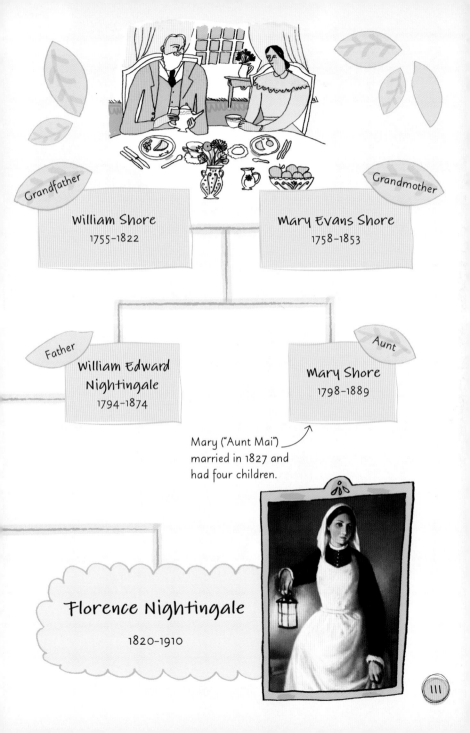

Grandfather

William Shore
1755–1822

Grandmother

Mary Evans Shore
1758–1853

Father

William Edward Nightingale
1794–1874

Aunt

Mary Shore
1798–1889

Mary ("Aunt Mai") married in 1827 and had four children.

Florence Nightingale

1820–1910

Timeline

A terrible flu epidemic hits England in January. Sixteen-year-old Florence helps nurse the sick in her household.

Florence Nightingale is born in Florence, Italy, on May 12, 1820.

Florence asks her parents for permission to become a nurse. They refuse.

1820

1837

1845

1846

Florence writes on February 7 that she has experienced a "call from God" to be of service to others.

Florence finds out about a place in Kaiserswerth, Germany, where she can study to become a nurse.

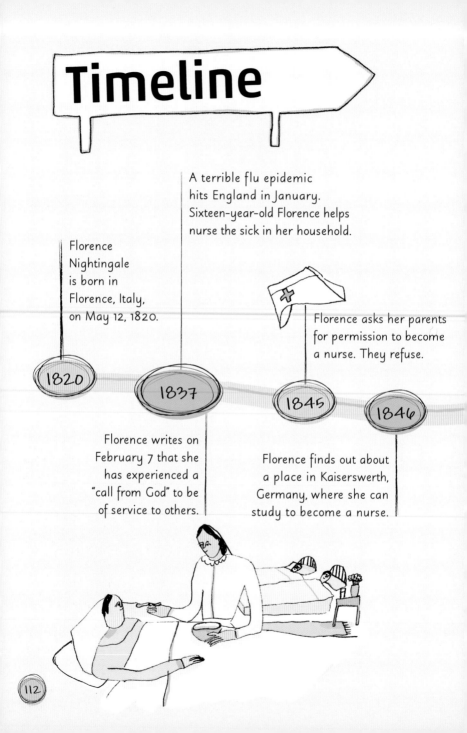

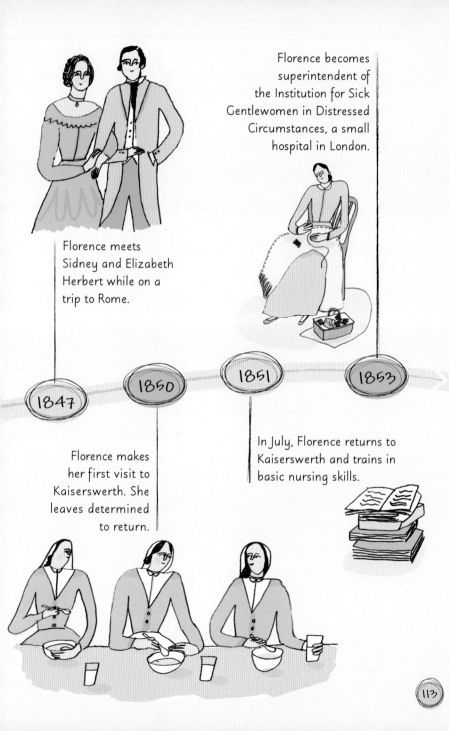

Florence meets Sidney and Elizabeth Herbert while on a trip to Rome.

Florence becomes superintendent of the Institution for Sick Gentlewomen in Distressed Circumstances, a small hospital in London.

1847

1850

1851

1853

Florence makes her first visit to Kaiserswerth. She leaves determined to return.

In July, Florence returns to Kaiserswerth and trains in basic nursing skills.

In October, Florence leads 38 other nurses on board a ship bound for Scutari to care for British soldiers during the Crimean War.

A treaty on March 30 ends the Crimean War. Florence returns home to England in August.

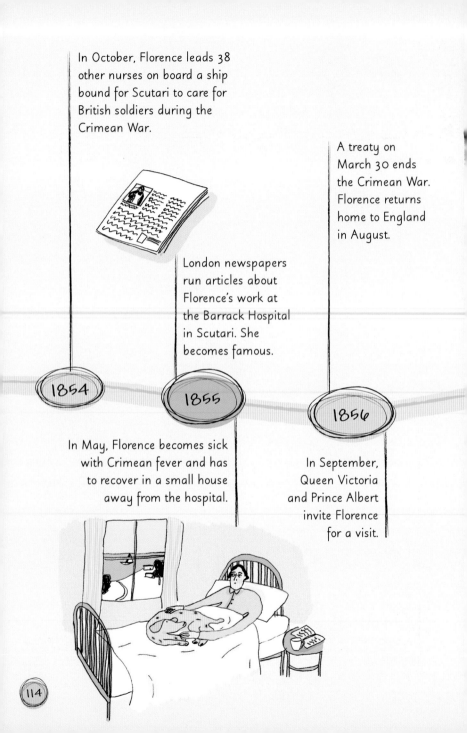

London newspapers run articles about Florence's work at the Barrack Hospital in Scutari. She becomes famous.

1854

1855

1856

In May, Florence becomes sick with Crimean fever and has to recover in a small house away from the hospital.

In September, Queen Victoria and Prince Albert invite Florence for a visit.

Florence is the first woman to be given the Order of Merit. (Another woman will not receive the honor until 1968.)

The US Civil War begins and is fought until 1865. Florence consults the US military on managing its field hospitals.

1860 1861 1881 1907 1910

The Army Nursing Service is established, making nurses an official part of the British army.

Florence dies in August. Her family respects her wishes for a simple burial and turns down an offer for an elaborate funeral at Westminster Abbey.

Florence publishes *Notes on Nursing*, a book nurses still refer to today.

Quiz

1. During which war did Florence Nightingale's nursing make her famous in England?

2. Florence was named after a city in which country?

3. What was the name of the sheepdog that young Florence nursed back to health?

4. How did Florence and her family travel to Europe in 1837?

5. In which city did Florence first meet Sidney and Elizabeth Herbert?

6. What did Florence name the owl she found on her 1850 travels?

7. To whom did Florence write a letter asking to lead nurses to Scutari?

Do you remember what you've read?
How many of these questions about
Florence's life can you answer?

 8 Why did Florence cut her hair short when she arrived at the Barrack Hospital?

 9 What did *The Times* call Florence in a February 1855 article?

 10 What did Florence fund using the money Queen Victoria gave her after the war?

 11 Which diagram did Florence create to display data about health care?

 12 What holiday is celebrated every year on Florence's birthday, May 12?

Answers on page 128

Who's who?

Athena
(1850–1854)
Florence's beloved pet owl

Bonham Carter, Henry
(1827–1921)
Florence's cousin to
whom she sometimes
wrote letters

Cap
(unknown)
sheepdog Florence nursed
back to health when she
was a teenager

Captain
(unknown)
one of Florence's pet dogs

Christie, Sara
(c.1800–1832)
Florence and Parthe's
childhood governess,
known to them as
"Miss Christie"

Herbert, Elizabeth
(1822–1911)
Florence's friend; married
to Sidney Herbert

Herbert, Sidney
(1810–1861)
Florence's friend; married
to Elizabeth Herbert; British
Secretary of State at War
from 1859–1861

MacDonald, John
(unknown)
war reporter for *The Times*
newspaper who called
Florence the "Lady with
the Lamp" in a 1855 article

Michaelangelo
(1475–1564)
Italian artist; Florence
admired his beautiful
religious paintings in
the Sistine Chapel

**Milnes, Richard
Monckton**
(1809–1885)
man who Florence's
parents hoped she
would marry; Florence
sometimes called him
her "poetic parcel"

Nightingale, Frances "Fanny"
(1788–1880)
Florence and Parthe's mother

Nightingale, Peter
(c.1737–1803)
William's great-uncle from whom he took over his estate and the last name Nightingale

Nightingale, William
(1794–1874)
Florence and Parthe's father; originally known as William Shore before changing his name in 1815

Peggie
(unknown)
Florence's pony

Peppercorn
(unknown)
one of Florence's pet dogs

Plato
(unknown–1850)
Florence's pet cicada; eaten by Athena the owl

Prince Albert
(1819–1861)
husband of Queen Victoria

Queen Victoria
(1819–1901)
Queen of the United Kingdom of Great Britain and Ireland from 1837–1901

Shore, Mary
(1798–1889)
Florence and Parthe's aunt, known to them as "Aunt Mai"

Teazer
(unknown)
one of Florence's pet dogs

Verney, Parthenope "Parthe"
(1819–1890)
Florence's sister

Verney, Sir Harry
(1801–1894)
Parthe's husband

Glossary

accomplish
to successfully
finish something

accomplished
good at doing something
or multiple things

activism
doing things to bring
about change

amputate
to cut off part of a
person or animal's body
for medical reasons

bonnet
type of hat that ties
under the chin

calling
work that someone
feels he or she is meant
to do

carriage
wheeled vehicle that
is pulled by a horse

charity
act of giving money,
food, or help to others

china
plates, bowls, and cups
made from baked clay

cloak
coat with no sleeves that
hangs around the neck

companion
person who accompanies
another for travel
or recreation

compress
folded cloth held to the
body to reduce pain

coxcomb
diagram Florence made
to show health-care data
in a visual way

cultivating
improving something
by practice or training

deaconess
woman with special
jobs in a church

dress a wound
to protect a cut or
injury with a clean pad
or bandage in order to
promote healing

efficiency
ability to do something
without waste

eligible
having the right
qualities for something,
such as marriage

empathy
ability to share another's
feelings

epidemic
illness that spreads
fast to a lot of people

famine
terrible food shortage

governess
woman employed to teach and care for children in the home

inappropriate
not right for a certain situation

inferior
lower in rank than something or someone else

needlepoint
embroidery

pioneer
first person to explore a new area

portrait
photograph, drawing, or painting of someone

precise
exact

profession
career

refine
to improve by making small changes

sanitize
to clean something well enough to prevent disease

smog
thick air pollution

soot
black powder that forms when coal or wood is burned

specimen
plant or animal collected for study

statistics
facts or pieces of information that help people understand something

steam packet
type of steamship

superintendent
manager or leader of an activity or organization

treaty
agreement between countries

turmoil
state of disturbance or confusion

tyranny
unfair treatment of people by those who have more power

Victorian
system of values and behavior modeled after those of the British Queen Victoria and Prince Albert

war reporter
journalist who travels to a war zone and shares stories about the war through news sources in their home country

war zone
region where a war is fought

Index

Acknowledgments

The author would like to thank Holly Carter-Chappell for consulting and sharing little-known details about Florence Nightingale; Charlotte Ager for her adorable illustrations; Allie Singer and everyone else who worked on this book; and Florence herself for being a model for women's rights.

DK would like to thank Rebekah Wallin for proofreading; Helen Peters for the index; Jolyon Goddard and Cécile Landau for additional editorial; and Radhika Banerjee for additional design.

The publisher would like to thank the following for their kind permission to reproduce their photographs:
(Key: a-above; b-below/bottom; c-center; f-far; l-left; r-right; t-top)
9 Wellcome Collection http://creativecommons.org/licenses/by/4.0/. 11 Getty Images: Bettmann. 13 Alamy Stock Photo: INTERFOTO. 17 Wellcome Collection http://creativecommons.org/licenses/by/4.0/. 26 Getty Images: Hulton Archive / Culture Club. 29 Getty Images: DEA Picture Library. 33 Getty Images: DEA / G. DAGLI ORTI. 35 Getty Images: Alessandro Vasari / Archivio Vasari / Mondadori Portfolio. 36 Getty Images: Hulton Archive / Rischgitz. 39 Getty Images: Universal Images Group / Photo 12. 41 Getty Images: Arkivi. 42 Alamy Stock Photo: eye35.pix. 46 Getty Images: Image by Lee Christensen. 47 Wellcome Collection http://creativecommons.org/licenses/by/4.0/. 55 Wellcome Collection http://creativecommons.org/licenses/by/4.0/. 61 Getty Images: Universal History Archive / UIG. 62 iStockphoto.com: duncan1890 / DigitalVision Vectors. 67 Mary Evans Picture Library. 70 Getty Images: Hulton Archive / Stringer.

74-75 Alamy Stock Photo: Peter Horree. 79 Getty Images: Print Collector / Hulton Archive. 80 Alamy Stock Photo: picture. 81 Alamy Stock Photo: Granger Historical Picture Archive. 88 Alamy Stock Photo: Pictures Now. 89 Bridgeman Images: National Army Museum, London. 90 Alamy Stock Photo: David Gee 4. 92 Getty Images: Culture Club / Hulton Archive. 95 Getty Images: Smith Collection / Gado / Archive Photos. 96 Wellcome Collection http://creativecommons.org/licenses/by/4.0/. 99 Alamy Stock Photo: ian macrae young. 103 Bridgeman Images: Florence Nightingale Museum, London, UK (bl). Courtesy of Florence Nightingale Museum, London: (bc). 105 Getty Images: Massimo Pizzotti. 106-107 Florence Nightingale Foundation: Ross Young Photography. 109 Bridgeman Images: Florence Nightingale Museum, London, UK. 111 Getty Images: Bettmann

Cover images: *Front and Spine*: Getty Images: Hulton Archive / Stringer

All other images © Dorling Kindersley
For further information see: www.dkimages.com

ANSWERS TO THE QUIZ ON PAGES 116–117

1. the Crimean War; 2. Italy; 3. Cap; 4. on a steam packet called the *Monarch*; 5. Rome, Italy; 6. Athena; 7. Elizabeth Herbert; 8. to keep it free from lice; 9. the "Lady with the Lamp"; 10. a hospital and a training school for nurses; 11. coxcomb diagram, or rose diagram; 12. International Nurses Day